to Understanding
What She
Really Means

A Man's Guide to Understanding What She Really Means

Susan H. Grant and Michael Levin

Andrews and McMeel
A Universal Press Syndicate Company
Kansas City

ISBN: 0-8362-2709-3

Library of Congress Catalog Card Number: 96-86636

*This book is dedicated
to any man who
wants to feel loved*

She Says:
I haven't seen my
(parents) family in a
long time.

She Means:

Will you go with me
while I visit my parents
and be loving, kind,
and patient?

*S*he *S*ays:

Can we afford to buy that car?

She Means:

I can't feel peaceful
about anything in our
life if we can't pay our
bills. Please be sure
we're considering my
comfort level too when
making this decision.

She Says:
I have a headache.
I'm sorry.

She Means:
I'm exhausted. Please
kiss me goodnight, be
my friend, and let me
go to sleep.

She Says:
I'm going to take a
little bath before I go
to sleep.

She Means:
If you can stay awake
for ten minutes longer
I'd like to make love
tonight.

She Says:

I hate to empty the dishwasher.

She Means:

I do so many things around the house, could you please do this one thing for me?

She Says:
I wish I could get a
manicure.

She Means:
I feel like I'm doing
so much for everyone
else. I wish I could do
something for myself.

She Says:
Would you please remember to put the toilet seat down.

She Means:
I don't ask for much; please be a little considerate of me.

She Says:

I have to arrive at work
by 7:30 this morning.

She Means:

I'm going to be rushed.
Could you help me
to do some of those
things for which I'm
responsible?

*S*he *S*ays:
I don't have dinner
ready. I'm sorry.

She Means:

Could we go out to get
something to eat tonight,
or could you fix dinner
for yourself without
saying something
which might cause me
to feel unworthy?

She Says:
You always have to be right.

She Means:
You haven't been listening to me and considering my perspective.

She Says:
Can I be alone while
I'm getting dressed?

She Means:
I'm a little self-
conscious about the
appearance of my body;
please be considerate
of how I'm feeling.

She Says:
I never know where
we stand when it
comes to money.

She Means:
You're not keeping
me informed, and I
feel vulnerable and
uncomfortable about it.

She Says:

Can't you do anything
around the house?

She Means:
This is your home too—helping me is "foreplay." Get it?

She Says:
I wish you'd try
harder to like my
brother (sister).

She Means:

I love my brother. I
want to share my life
with him too; don't
make it hard for me
to be with him.

She Says:

Did you make the deposit?

She Means:
Tell me that we are
okay financially and
that I shouldn't worry
about writing a check
at the grocery store.

She Says:
Can you please tell
(child's name) to clean
up his/her room?

$\mathcal{S}$he $\mathcal{M}$eans:
I'm always telling
(child's name) to do
things. I don't always
want to seem to be the
bad guy. Please say
something to him/her.

She Says:
(Child's name) isn't
doing very well in
science.

She Says:
Honey. Why don't you
take some time and
take a shower?

She Means:
Please share in the
responsibility of helping
him/her.

*S*he *S*ays:
(Child's name) has to
go to the library. I'm
going to drive him/her.

*S*he *M*eans:
Would you please drive
him/her for me, or
would you go with me
to keep me company?

*S*he *S*ays:
Did you pay the ℓ
bill?

*S*he *M*eans:
I hope I don't have
to feel embarrassed
because our phone
may be shut off.

*S*he *M*eans:

I want to find you
attractive and easy to
be with. If you're not
clean I can't feel that
way.

*S*he *S*ays:
Do you have to drink
so many beers (drinks)?

She Means:
You frighten me when
you drink so much. It
makes me feel like you
are avoiding being
with me and not deal-
ing with life very well.

She Says:

I love the way you smell.

She Means:
Wear that fragrance again.

She Says:

Could you please stop interrupting me?

She $Means:$
You are not allowing
me to tell you what I'm
thinking and feeling.
When you interrupt
me I feel like you
don't care about my
perspective.

She Says:
You don't appreciate
anything I do.

She Means:
I don't feel worthy
when I'm in your
presence.

She Says:
This house is a mess.

She Means:
Please help me clean
the house or let me
know it's okay to have
a service to clean once
a week.

She Says:

Don't get into the car before I'm ready to leave.

She Means:
You're rushing me too much before we're leaving to go someplace. I may forget to do something important because I feel rushed. And oh, yes, why don't you ask me if there's anything you can do?

She Says:

I feel so bloated.

She Means:
I'm either about to
begin menstruating
or I am menstruating.
Please treat me with
a little more patience
and understanding.

She Says:
I think those pictures
in *Playboy* are
disgusting.

She Means:

She's nineteen years old. She spends all day working out and primping for photo shoots. I'm thirty or forty something. I've had (one, two, three) kids. I work all day. I take care of the kids, house, and you. How can you be so insensitive to my feelings by gloating over her?

She Says:
I'm exhausted.

She Means:
Give me my space and
do anything that needs
to be done around the
house so I don't have
to think about it.

She Says:

Do you have to stay up so late at night?

She Means:

I'd love to be lying next to you being peaceful and quiet while we fall asleep together. I need that tonight.

She Says:
I'm cold.

She Means:
Put your arm around
me or get me a jacket
or do something for
me like you would
have done before we
made a commitment to
each other.

She Says:
I have a headache.

She Means:
Can you get me something for my headache and a glass of water?

She Says:
Do you have to yell?

She Means:
Your yelling makes me
feel like you are trying
to intimidate me.

She Says:

I don't expect you to
read my mind.

She Means:
I expect you to listen
to my words carefully,
look at my eyes when
we're speaking to each
other, and be sensitive
to my body language.

She Says:
You don't look at me
when you're talking to
me.

She Means:
I feel like you are
being impersonal when
you speak to me.

She Says:
Do you have to drive
so fast?

She Means:
You seem to be driving
carelessly, and I'm
scared.

She Says:

I thought you were
going to be home by
6:00.

She Means:
I need to be able to
trust that you'll keep
commitments, even if
it involves being home
when you say you will.

She Says:
You're always working.

She Means:
You're breaking your promise to make sure I feel loved. You need to try to create a better balance between work and our relationship.

She Says:
[...]on't have enough
[...]e during the day.

She Means:
[...]eed you to try and
[...]p me absorb some of
[...]e responsibilities that
[...] normally burdened
[...]h each day.

She Says:
You're never wrong.

She Means:
You don't seem to
consider my feelings
and thoughts. Soon I
won't share myself
with you unless you
become more open to
my opinions.

She Says:
I'm under so much
pressure at work.

She Means:
I need you to
that it's only
that my best
enough, and
you to hold n

She Says:
The dust seems to
build up so quickly.

She Means:
Help me clean the
house, please.

She Says:
I know this isn't your favorite meal.

She Means:
Tell me that anything I've made is good enough and that you appreciate that I prepared the meal.

She Says:
I have to go grocery
shopping.

She Means:
Would you go with me
to keep me company?

She Says:

My car seems out of alignment and pulls to the right.

She Means:
Please take care of
whatever the problem
is with my stupid car
so I don't have to think
about it and so I know
you worry about my
safety.

She Says:
All you ever do is talk
about your work.

She Means:

You never ask about my day or if I'm feeling or doing okay, you just expect me to be there to listen to you and be supportive. My needs are not being fulfilled.

She Says:
Do you have to start watching TV immediately after dinner?

She $Means:$

It seems that you'll
do anything just to
distance yourself from
sharing our leisure
time together.

She Says:
Do you still love me?

She Means:
Do you still care about my feelings as much as you care about your own?

She Says:
You don't care about
my feelings.

She Means:
I'm feeling as though
you don't love me.

She Says:
You're being so defensive anytime I tell you how I feel.

She Means:
You're exhibiting a pattern of behavior that is preventing you from seeing the truth of what I'm feeling about our relationship.

She Says:
Why don't you spend
some time with the
children?

*S*he *M*eans:

You're too preoccupied
with both work and your
own personal needs. We
all need to share more
time with you.

—➤●◄—

*S*he *S*ays:
When it comes to
having sex all you care
about is yourself.

—➤●◄—

She Means:
Where is it written that
you're the only one
who should experience
the pleasure of sex?

She Says:
Nothing I ever do is
good enough.

She Means:
I don't feel worthy in your presence. I feel like I have to be careful to do everything just as you like or you'll criticize me. I need you to compliment me.

*S*he *S*ays:
You're not the person
I married.

She Means:
Before we were married
you made promises,
some of which you ver-
balized and others that
you didn't verbalize,
but implied from your
behavior. You are
breaking those promises
to me.

She Says:

I feel like life is passing me by.

She Means:
I've either lost or am
losing my own individ-
uality because I've
given all of myself to
you and our family.
I'm becoming impa-
tient to begin doing
things for myself now.

She Says:

I can't tell you how I really feel.

She Means:

I don't trust you.
When I try to tell you
how I feel you either
don't listen or try to
make me feel that I'm
wrong or shouldn't
feel that way.

She Says:
You are always doing
things for other people.

She Means:
I feel like you prefer
to show everyone else
how wonderful you
are but care little
about my feelings and
comfort level.

She Says:
I'm not perfect.

She Means:
You are being so critical
of me that I am feeling
uneasy just being in
your presence.

She Says:
Why do you have to
pay so much attention
to "her"?

She Means:
When you pay so much
attention to "her" I
feel replaceable, and it
makes me feel afraid.

She Says:
You always sound like
you are angry with me.

She Means:
I feel like you are try-
ing to control me with
what appears to be an
ongoing attitude of
apparent disapproval.

───➤◆◄───

She Says:
Thank you for being
perceptive.

She Means:
Exactly what she says.

───➤◆◄───